Famous People

ALEXANDER GRAHAM BELL
1847~1922

Christine Moorcroft
Magnus Magnusson

Christine Moorcroft is an educational consultant and an Ofsted inspector, who was a teacher in primary and special schools and a lecturer in education. She has written and edited several books on history and religion and on other subjects, including personal and social education, science and English.

Magnus Magnusson KBE, has written several books on history and archaeology, and translated many Icelandic sagas and modern Icelandic novels. He has presented major television programmes on history and archaeology, such as *Chronicle*, *The Archaeology of the Bible Lands* and *Living Legends*, as well as the long-running quiz series, *Mastermind*. He is currently chairman of Scottish Natural Heritage, the Government body which advises on environmental issues.

4 LEARNING

ACKNOWLEDGEMENTS

The authors thank the following for their help: Eddie Birch (British Telecom) Roger Bridgman (Curator, Telecommunications, Science Museum), the staff of Childwall Library, Liverpool.

Picture credits
Science Museum: pages 4, 6, 17 (both)
Hulton: page 19
R A J Earl: page 14
British Telecom: pages 8, 16

Published by Channel Four Learning Limited
Castle House
75–76 Wells Street
London W1P 3RE

© 1998 Channel Four Learning

All rights reserved.

Written by Christine Moorcroft and Magnus Magnusson
Illustrated by Rodney Sutton
Cover illustration by Jeffrey Burn
Designed by Blade Communications
Edited by Margot O'Keeffe
Printed by Alden Press
ISBN 1-86215-348-5

For further information about Channel 4 Schools and details of published materials, contact
Channel 4 Schools
PO Box 100
Warwick CV34 6TZ
Tel: 01926 436444
Fax: 01926 436446

Contents

Childhood 4

Growing up 6

Learning to teach speech 8

Teaching deaf people 10

A new life in North America 12

The telephone 14

The first telephone exchange 16

A lifetime of inventions 18

Time-lines 20

How to find out more 22

Glossary 23

Index 24

Childhood

Alexander Graham Bell was born in 1847 in Edinburgh. His family called him Aleck. He had two brothers: Melville ('Melly'), who was two years older than him, and Edward ('Ted'), who was a year younger.

Aleck's family was very interested in speech and hearing. His mother, Eliza, was almost deaf. She could hear Aleck's voice, though, because it was strong and clear. His father, Alexander Melville Bell, was a professor of elocution at Edinburgh University.

Aleck's grandfather was also interested in speech and hearing. He helped people in London who had problems with their speech.

Aleck's mother taught him at home until he went to school at the age of ten. He could play the piano when he was very young and had lessons from a famous pianist.

People who could not hear well used a hearing-trumpet.

Aleck enjoyed inventing things. His best friend was Ben Herdman, whose father owned a flour mill. One day, when the two boys were at the mill, Mr Herdman said that instead of playing they should do something useful.

"What should we do?" asked Aleck. Mr Herdman said that the most useful thing they could do was to find an easy way to take the husks off grains of wheat. He did not really think they could do it.

But they did! The boys found that they could scrub off the husks using a nail brush, but this took a long time. Then they remembered seeing an old vat with a paddle wheel inside it. They covered the inside of the vat with rough bristles and turned the paddle-wheel. It worked! The husks were scrubbed away!

Did you know?

- *In Bell's time there were no hearing aids like those we have today.*

- *Deaf people would put a hearing-trumpet to one ear. The wide part collected the sounds, which vibrated along the tube to the person's ear.*

5

Growing up

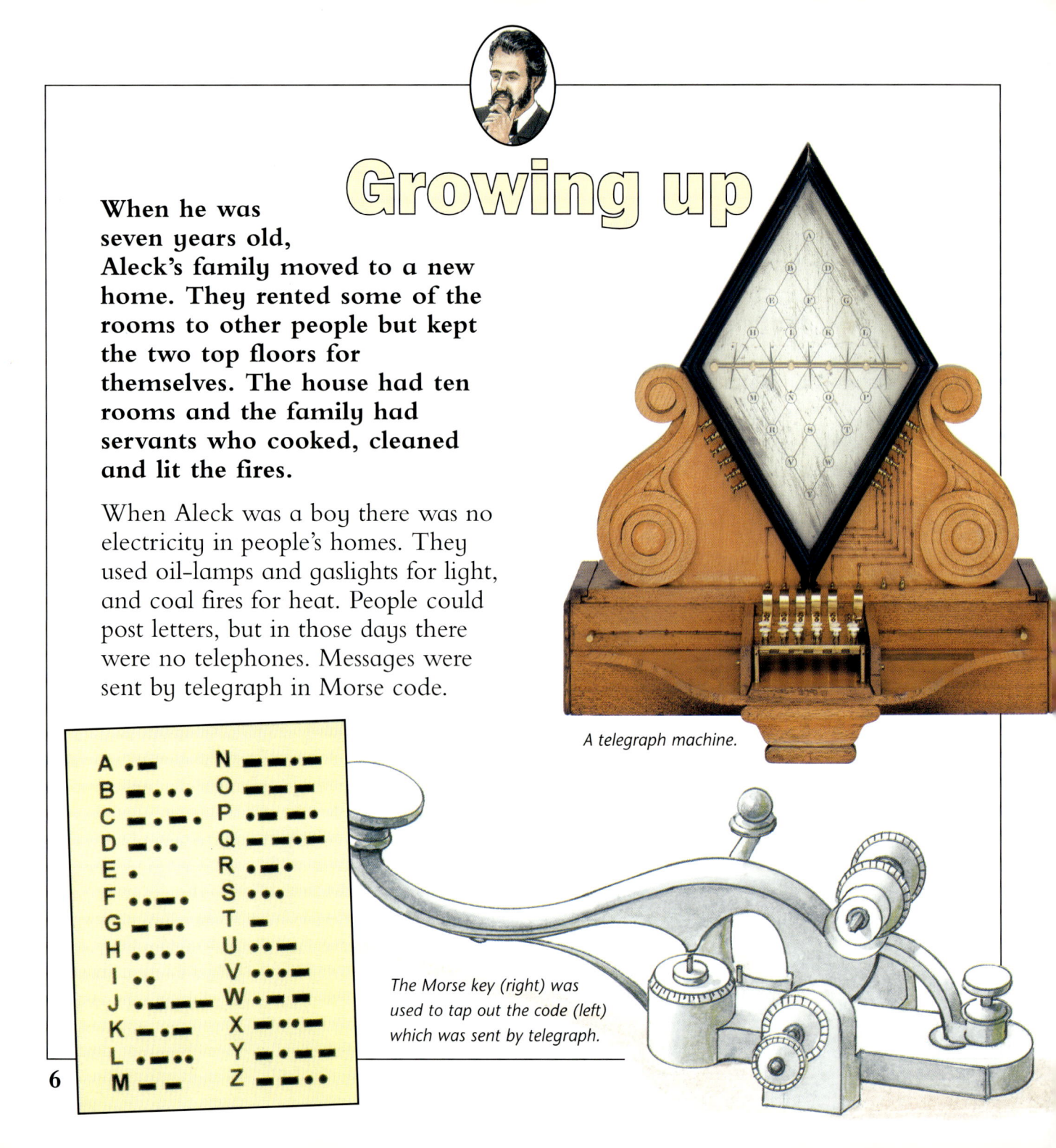

When he was seven years old, Aleck's family moved to a new home. They rented some of the rooms to other people but kept the two top floors for themselves. The house had ten rooms and the family had servants who cooked, cleaned and lit the fires.

When Aleck was a boy there was no electricity in people's homes. They used oil-lamps and gaslights for light, and coal fires for heat. People could post letters, but in those days there were no telephones. Messages were sent by telegraph in Morse code.

A telegraph machine.

The Morse key (right) was used to tap out the code (left) which was sent by telegraph.

Aleck's father had invented a way of writing down all the sounds the human voice could make. He wanted to use this to teach deaf people to read, write and speak. Lots of people came to see how it worked. Aleck was very good at reading the symbols. He helped his father to show people how it worked.

Sometimes, while Aleck waited outside the room, his father asked someone to make unusual sounds with his or her voice. Then he drew a symbol for each sound on the board and asked Aleck to come into the room. Aleck would look at the symbols and make the sounds.

People thought Professor Bell and his son were very clever.

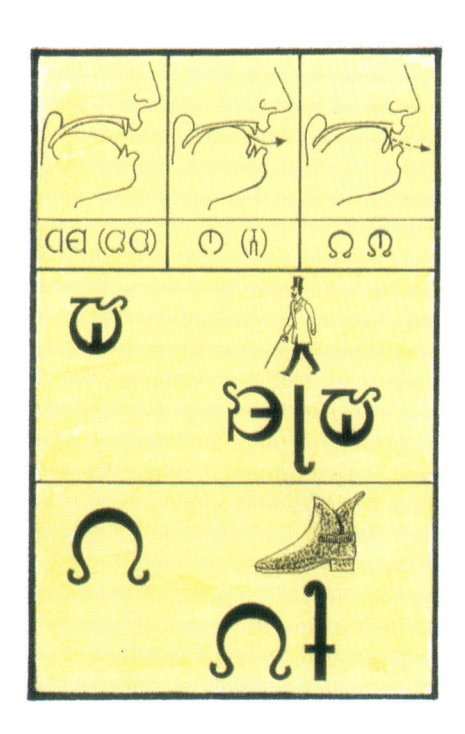

Above are some of the pictures and their sounds, used for teaching deaf people to speak.

Did you know?

- **The Penny Post started in 1840. It cost a penny to send a letter. Letters were carried by stage-coach, train and steamship.**

- **William Cooke and Charles Wheatstone had invented the electric telegraph. It was first used in 1838.**

- **The telegraph was quicker than the Penny Post, but very expensive.**

- **Morse code was named after its inventor, Samuel Morse.**

Learning to teach speech

When he was 13, Aleck went to stay in London with his grandfather. He met Sir Charles Wheatstone, the man who had invented the telegraph, and saw his 'talking machine' which could copy the human voice.

Aleck and his brother Melly decided to build a talking machine of their own. They had to make a tongue, a mouth with lips, some lungs and a larynx (the part which makes the sound).

They made them out of tin, rubber and pieces of cotton. They joined them up so that they moved in the right way. Then for the test!

Melly blew air through a tin tube while Aleck moved the mouth and tongue. The sound which came out was not quite right, so they made some changes. Finally it made a sound, like a baby crying "Mama"!

Sir Charles Wheatstone

Making this machine taught Aleck to keep trying when things were difficult. He also learned a lot about how the voice works and, he said, "It started me along the path which led to the telephone".

Aleck also taught his dog to speak! The dog growled while Aleck moved its mouth. The dog enjoyed all the fuss so much that it would try to talk without Aleck's help!

About this time, Aleck went to Weston House School in Elgin to learn Latin and Greek and to teach speech and music.

Aleck would hold the dog's mouth and move its lips while it growled. He learned to move the dog's mouth so that it could make different sounds. It could say "How are you, Grandmama?"

Did you know?

- Aleck's pupils at Weston House did very well. A local newspaper reported how well even the youngest children spoke.
- Aleck went on to Edinburgh University, but was more interested in helping his father with his work on speech.

Teaching deaf people

Aleck's father was still finding out about the ways in which sounds are made with the voice. He wanted to be able to teach deaf people to speak. He asked Aleck to listen to some sounds being whispered. Could he hear a musical scale?

Aleck could hear it, and he even found a way to measure the pitch of the sounds using tuning-forks.

At this time, Aleck was teaching in London. He was often ill but when he was 20 he moved to Bath and his health became better. Sadly, his brother Ted died when he was only 18 years old.

Then Aleck went back to London to study. As an experiment, he used his father's symbols to teach some deaf children. He was very successful. The children soon learned to make all the sounds!

Aleck taught his deaf pupils to understand how speech works by feeling the vibrations made by their own voices. This helped them to make the right sounds.

One day, Aleck read a book by a German scientist about a tuning-fork sounder he had invented. This machine used electro-magnets to make tuning-forks keep vibrating.

This gave Aleck the idea that electricity could be used to carry sounds. He wanted to learn more about electricity. He told his friends that one day they would talk to one another by telegraph.

A tuning-fork

Did you know?

- *At this time, some scientists were finding out how electricity could be made.*
- *Other scientists were investigating ways of recording the human voice. Thomas Edison was one of these scientists. He invented the gramophone (the first record player).*

A new life in North America

In 1870 Aleck's brother Melly, who was only 25, died. He was the second of Aleck's brothers to die. Aleck's father was very sad and he decided to take his family to live in Canada.

By this time, Aleck was grown up. He went to work in the United States of America, where he taught deaf children. Each summer he went back to Canada to stay with his parents. He was very happy when he taught a deaf child to talk.

Aleck was also still investigating his idea for sending sounds along wires. He ran wires to his next-door neighbour's house. His neighbour could hear a tiny sound.

One of Aleck's deaf pupils was George Sanders who was five years old. Aleck taught him the alphabet using a glove marked with the letters of the alphabet. He would point to the letters which spelled the words he was saying.

Another of Aleck's deaf pupils was 16-year-old Mabel Hubbard. Her father was very rich.

One day, Aleck noticed that when he sang a note into a piano, while pressing its pedal, the wires inside it vibrated and made the same sound. He thought he could make the wires repeat all the sounds of a word and a sentence. He was very excited!

Aleck showed Mr Hubbard, Mabel's father, the piano trick. He told Mr Hubbard about his ideas for the talking telegraph. Mr Hubbard was very interested. He talked to Mr Sanders, George's father, and they agreed to pay Aleck to invent the talking telegraph.

Did you know?

- *Other people were trying to make talking telegraphs.*

- *Mr Hubbard and Mr Sanders wanted Aleck to spend all his time working on his telegraph. But Aleck wanted to teach his pupils. He worked on it only in the evenings and at weekends.*

The telephone

Aleck worked hard on his idea for the 'telephone'. Before long he knew he would be able to make a machine which would let people talk to one another across long distances.

In 1874, he met a man called Thomas Watson, who worked in the electrical shop where he bought the things he needed for his inventions. Thomas understood electricity, so Aleck asked him to be his assistant.

They set up the machines in the electrical shop. The story goes that in July 1875, Aleck was working on the machine upstairs when he knocked some liquid on to the table.

The telephone which Alexander Graham Bell made with Thomas Watson.

14

He shouted into his machine "Mr Watson, come here quickly." Thomas, who was downstairs, heard a sound come through the machine! It worked! The next step was to make the voices sound clearer. On 10 March 1876, Aleck spoke into the machine and at the other end of the wire Thomas could hear what he said.

Aleck wrote to his father to tell him the good news. He knew that one day soon people would be able to talk to one another without leaving their homes.

All this time, other people had been trying to invent a telephone. But Alexander Graham Bell was the first to do it.

Did you know?

- Aleck wrote to the United States Patent Office about his invention. He called it an 'autograph telegraph'.

- Another man, Elisha Gray, had also invented a telephone. He called his a 'teleautograph'.

The first telephone exchange

In the summer of 1876 Aleck went to Canada to stay with his parents. But he was still thinking about his invention. He bought lots of wire and, using a cart, ran wires from his parents' home to a building in the town.

The farmers who helped him thought he was mad. He fixed a telephone to each end of the wire. Then he tested them. They worked! He could hear what someone was saying at the other end of the wire!

A telephone switchboard. At first boys and young men worked on switchboards but soon nearly all operators were women, because telephone operators found this made callers more polite.

Soon Gardiner Hubbard, the father of Aleck's pupil, Mabel, set up a telephone company. People paid the company to put up telephone wires and they rented the telephones. Then telephones were set up in other towns. Before long, American towns had lots of telephone wires.

In 1877, Alexander married Mabel Hubbard. They went to England for their honeymoon, and there Aleck showed Queen Victoria his telephone. She asked him to put one in her home in the Isle of Wight.

Alexander Graham Bell at the time of the first telephone.

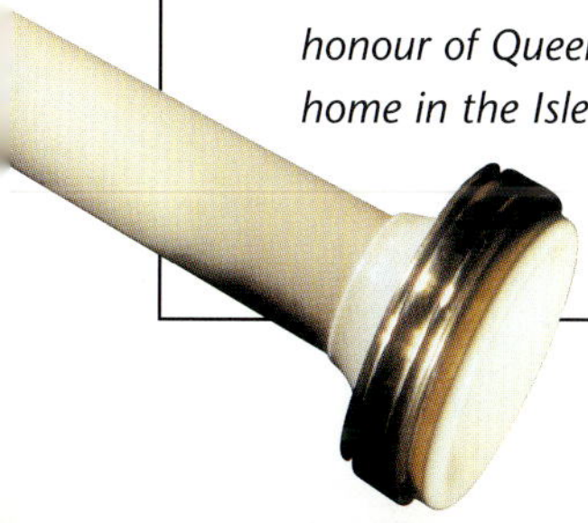

The Bell Osborne telephone, dated 1878. It was named in honour of Queen Victoria's home in the Isle of Wight.

Did you know?

- **The first telephones from Hubbard's company could only be used for distances of up to 32 km.**

- **To make a telephone call you picked up your telephone. This rang a bell at the telephone exchange. The operator asked whom you wanted to call. He used a switch to join your telephone wire to that of the other person.**

- **There were no telephone numbers. The operators knew each customer by name!**

A lifetime of inventions

Aleck was more interested in his inventions than in running a telephone business. He wondered whether telephones could be made to work without wires! He began work on a 'photophone' which would use a beam of light instead of wires.

Then, in 1881, two events changed his work. In July, President James Garfield was shot. But the doctors could not find the bullet inside him. Aleck set to work to make a metal-detector which would help them.

Also, Aleck and his wife had a baby boy, Edward. Sadly, the baby died because he could not breathe properly. So Aleck started work on a machine which could help people to breathe.

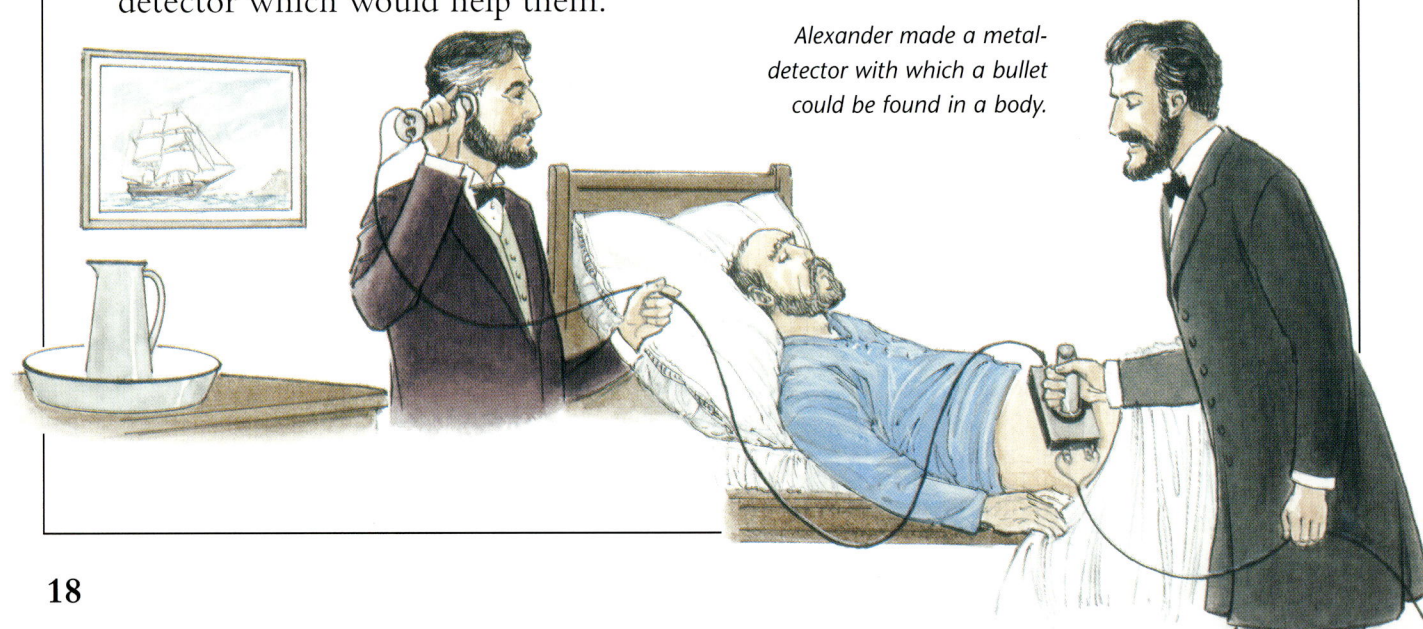

Alexander made a metal-detector with which a bullet could be found in a body.

Alexander invented many more things, including a wax disc on which to record voices, an electric heater, a solar heater, one kite with solar panels and another which could carry one person. He experimented with flight, X-rays, hydrofoils and recycling heat energy.

Aleck was always sad that deaf people could not use his great invention, the telephone. He died on 2 August 1922 and was buried in the grounds of the family's home in Nova Scotia, in Canada.

Alexander Graham Bell in 1910 at the age of 63.

Did you know?

- *In 1879 Bell invented the audiometer. This measured how well people could hear.*

- *The decibel, the unit for measuring sound, was named after him.*

- *He started a school for training teachers to teach deaf children. One of his teachers, Annie Sullivan, taught the deaf and blind Helen Keller. Helen became a world-famous writer and lecturer.*

Time-lines

1847 — Alexander Graham Bell was born

1862 — With his brother, Melly, he made a 'talking machine'

1873 — He began working on his telegraph

1876 — He sent the first clear telephone message

---

500 BC

55 — Julius Caesar invaded Britain

c30 — Jesus was crucified

0

c570 — Muhammad was born

AD 500

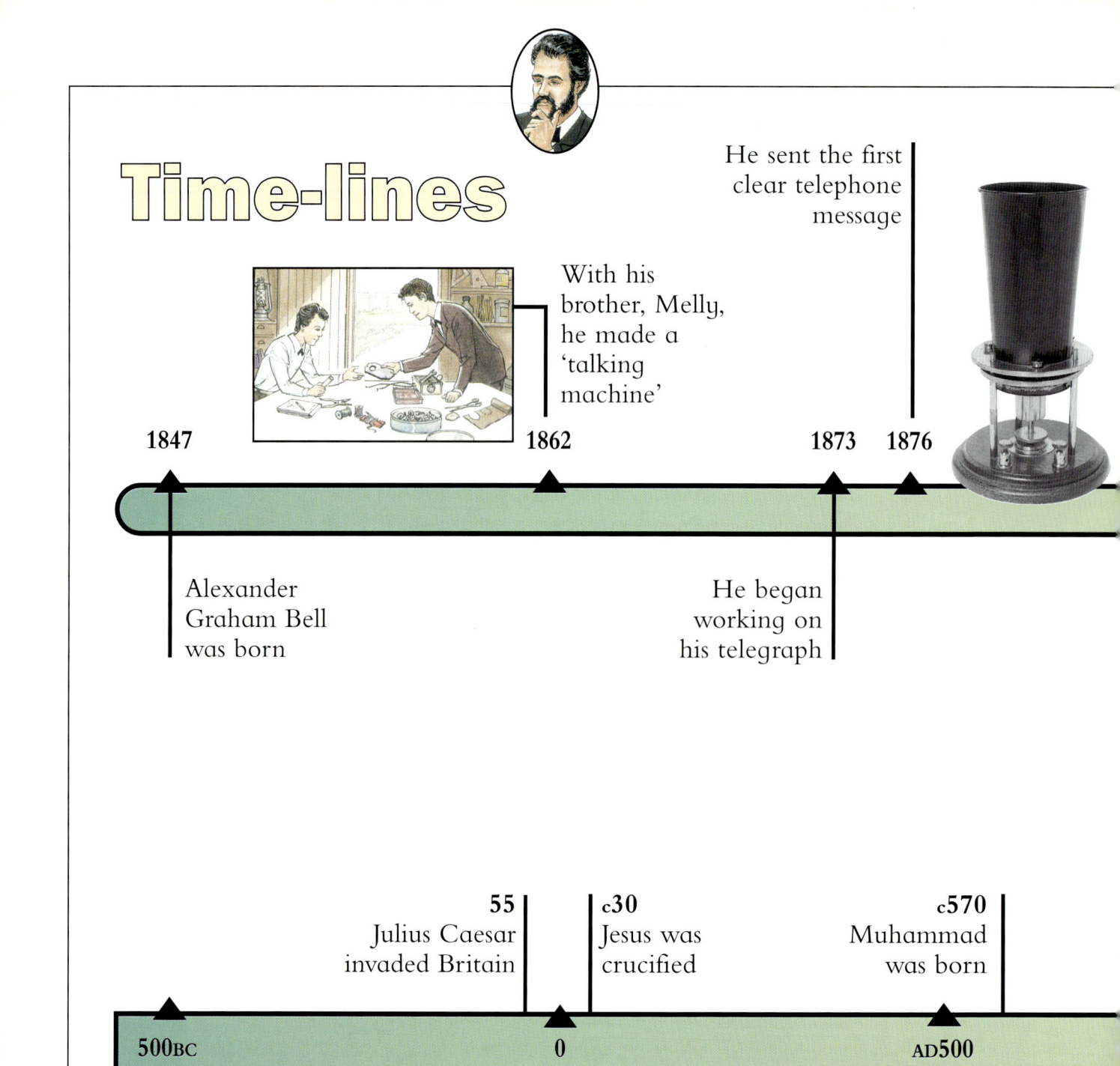

20

Bell designed a solar heater

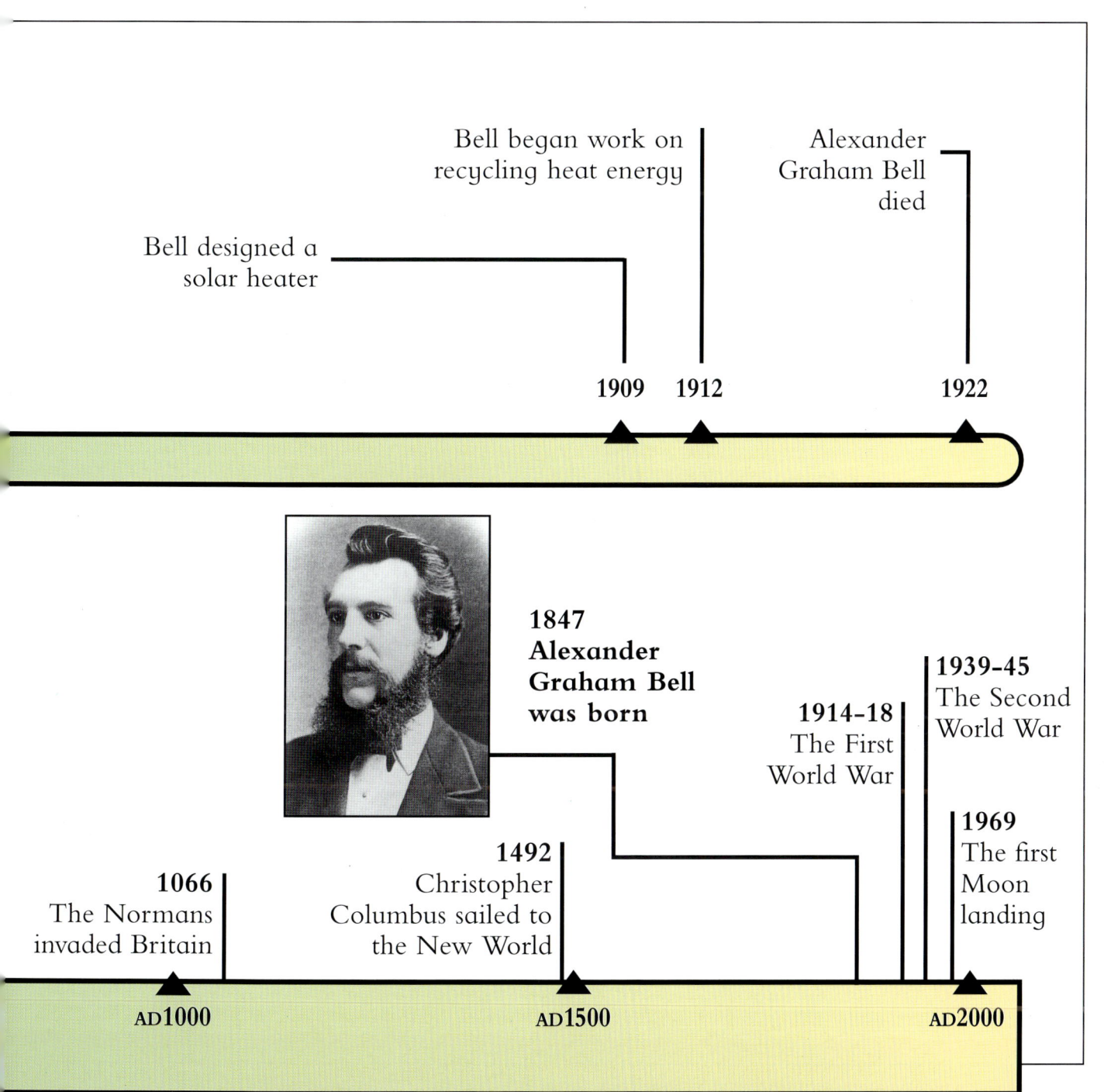

Bell began work on recycling heat energy

Alexander Graham Bell died

1909   1912   1922

1847 Alexander Graham Bell was born

1492 Christopher Columbus sailed to the New World

1914-18 The First World War

1939-45 The Second World War

1969 The first Moon landing

1066 The Normans invaded Britain

AD1000   AD1500   AD2000

How to find out more

More books to read

Alexander Graham Bell: The Life and Times of the Man Who Invented the Telephone by Edwin S Grosvenor & Morgan Wesson (Harry Abrams, 1997).

Sounds Out of Silence: A Life of Alexander Graham Bell by James Mackay (Mainstream Publishing, 1997)

Old Telephones by Andrew Emmerson (Shire Publications, 1994)

Bell: Alexander Graham Bell & The Conquest of Solitude by Robert V Bruce (Victor Gollancz, 1973).

Alexander Graham Bell by Steve Parker (Belitha Press, 1994)

Inventors by Struan Reid and Patricia Farar (Usborne, 1994)

Alexander Graham Bell by Andrew Dunn (Wayland, 1990)

Alexander Graham Bell by Richard Tames (Franklin Watts, 1990)

Television programmes to watch

Channel 4 Schools series, Stop Look, Listen: Famous People. Telephone 01926 436444.

Places to visit

Museum of Communication, 58 Union Street, Bo'ness, West Lothian, EH51 9QA.
Tel 01506 824507

Royal Museums of Scotland,
Chambers Street, Edinburgh,
Tel 0131 225 7534.

Science Museum, Exhibition Road,
London SW7 2DD.
Tel 0171 938 8000.

Story of Telecommunications,
135 Queen Victoria Street, London, EC4V 4AT.
Tel 0171 248 7444.

Places to which to write

Alexander Graham Bell Museum,
Baddeck, Nova Scotia, Canada.
Tel 001 902 295 2069.

Glossary

audiometer *(19)* A machine for measuring how well people can hear.

electro-magnet *(11)* A magnet made using electricity.

decibel *(19)* A unit for measuring sound.

elocution *(4)* Speaking. Elocution teachers teach people to speak clearly and with expression.

gramophone *(11)* An old-fashioned record-player.

hearing-trumpet *(4)* A tool which helped people to hear.

husk *(5)* The hard outside covering of a grain of wheat.

hydrofoil *(19)* A boat which lifts and skims across the water.

metal-detector *(18)* A machine which tells us if there is metal near it.

Morse code *(6)* A code of dots (short sounds) and dashes (long sounds) for letters of the alphabet.

operator *(16)* A person at the telephone exchange who connected telephone lines.

paddle-wheel *(5)* A wheel with wide, flat spokes.

patent *(15)* A document which allows one person to make or sell an invention.

pitch *(10)* The pitch of a sound describes how high or low it is.

scale *(10)* Musical notes arranged in a sort of ladder going up or down.

solar *(19)* Of the Sun.

switchboard *(16)* A machine which connects telephone lines.

symbol *(7)* A sign which is drawn or written.

telegraph *(6)* A machine which sends and receives coded messages.

telephone exchange *(17)* A building in which many telephone switchboards connect telephone lines for large areas.

tuning-fork *(10)* A metal fork which vibrates to the pitch of only one note.

vat *(5)* A big tub.

vibrate *(10)* To move to and fro.

Index

audiometer, 19
Bath, 10
Bell, Alexander Melville (Bell's father), 4, 7, 10, 12, 15
Bell, Edward (Ted) (Bell's younger brother), 4, 10
Bell, Melville (Melly) (Bell's elder brother), 4, 8, 12
Canada, 12, 16, 19
Cooke, William, 7
deafness, 4, 5, 7, 9, 10, 12, 19
decibel, 19
Edinburgh, 4, 9
Edison, Thomas, 11
electricity, 6, 11, 14
electro-magnet, 12
elocution, 4
Garfield, James, President of the USA, 18
gramophone, 11
Gray, Elisha, 15
hearing-trumpet, 4, 5
Herdman, Ben, 5
Hubbard, Gardiner Greene, 13, 17, 18
Hubbard, Mabel, (Bell's pupil and, later, wife), 13, 17, 18
hydrofoil, 19

Keller, Helen, 19
kite, 19
London, 4, 7, 10
metal-detector, 18
Morse code, 6, 7
operator, 16, 17
patent, 15
Penny Post, 7
piano, 4, 13
photophone, 18
pitch, 10
Sanders, George, 13
Sanders, Thomas, 13, 18
speech, 4, 8, 10
Sullivan, Annie, 19
switchboard, 16, 17
symbols, 7
talking machine, 8, 9
telegraph, 6, 7, 8, 11, 13, 15
telephone, 6, 9, 14, 15, 16, 17, 18, 19
telephone exchange, 16, 17
tuning-fork, 11, 12
United States of America, 12, 15
vibration, 10, 13
Victoria, Queen, 17
Watson, Thomas, 14, 15
Wheatstone, Sir Charles, 7, 8